Big Activities
for Little Hands
Winter

Written and illustrated by
Veronica Terrill

Cover by Veronica Terrill

Copyright © 1993, Good Apple

ISBN No. 0-86653-752-X

Printing No. 15 14 13 12 11

Good Apple
A Division of Frank Schaffer Publications, Inc.
23740 Hawthorne Boulevard
Torrance, CA 90505-5927

Dedication

With love, for my grandmother:
Agnes Veronica Wygant.
Thanks for tea parties, quilts and
always being there for me.

Table of Contents

Snowman 1

Snowflakes 3

Igloo 4

Penguin 5

My Mittens 7

Thermometer 9

Gingerbread Boy 10

Gingerbread Girl 11

Gingerbread House 12

Candy Cane 13

Stocking 14

Christmas Tree 15

Wreath 16

Toy Bag 17

Reindeer 19

Santa Stand-up 21

"Welcome, Santa" Door Hanger 22

Cookies for Santa 23

Santa Letter 24

Mini Holiday Cards 25

Hanukkah Poster and Dreidel Chain 27

Kwanzaa 29

New Year's Party 30

Chinese New Year Dragon Mask 31

Chinese New Year Puppet 32

Martin Luther King, Jr. 33

Lincoln and Washington Stick Puppets 34

Washington and Lincoln Mini Books 35

Groundhog Day 36

Happy Valentine 38

Pocketful of Love 39

Valentine Holder 41

Award 42

Newsletter/Parent Border 43

File Folder Cover 44

GA1467

Introduction

Big Activities for Little Hands: Winter is a terrific classroom companion to your winter curriculum. Inside the pages of *Big Activities for Little Hands: Winter* are wonderful seasonal projects that even your youngest preschooler will be able to proudly complete. The reproducible activity patterns were specifically designed with bold outlines and easy-to-cut shapes. Practicing vital color, cut and paste skills is made fun and enjoyable, as children create adorable winter room decorations and take-home projects. The activity pages are adaptable to the skill level of the child and often can be completed with little or no teacher assistance. Patterns may be precut so beginning preschoolers can assemble these seasonal projects with their crayons and a few dabs of paste. Children will love how "professional" their finished masterpieces will look. Celebrating winter in your classroom has never been so easy!

Helpful Hints

Use copy machines or overhead projectors to customize the patterns. Enlarge the Christmas tree pattern (page 15) to 60" (1.52 m) tall. Give each student a 4" (10.16 cm) circle of paper "ornament" to decorate. Attach all the circles to the tree along with tinsel or garland to create a classroom Christmas tree. Reduce the stocking pattern (page 14) to 4" (10.16 cm) tall and create Christmas name tags.

Use the projects in *Big Activities for Little Hands: Winter* to create student-made bulletin boards. Have children make the penguins (pages 5 and 6) and attach to a blue-covered bulletin board to create an icy winter scene.

Have fun with your choice of paper. Many copy or printing shops offer a variety of colors and textures to choose from. Copy the gingerbread boy and girl patterns (pages 10 and 11) on heavy, brown paper. Decorate with glue and white or crystal glitter. Add clothes made from scraps of Christmas wrapping paper.

Be creative with special touches. Use glitter, bits of ribbon and yarn or even sequins or wiggly eyes to add excitement to the finished projects. Outline the snowflakes (page 3) with glue and sprinkle with silver glitter. Glue small wiggly eyes over the existing eyes.

GA1467

Snowman

Reproduce the patterns on this page and page 2. Color and cut out on the heavy outlines. Paste snowman sections together as illustrated.

1

GA1467

Snowman

2

GA1467

Snowflakes

Reproduce the patterns below. Cut out on heavy outlines and decorate with dabs of glue and sprinkle with crystal or silver glitter. Paste decorated snowflakes on 8¹⁄₂" x 11" (21.6 x 27.94 cm) light blue construction paper.

Note: Tape finished snowflakes to short pieces of string and tie to drinking straws to create a "snowflake mobile."

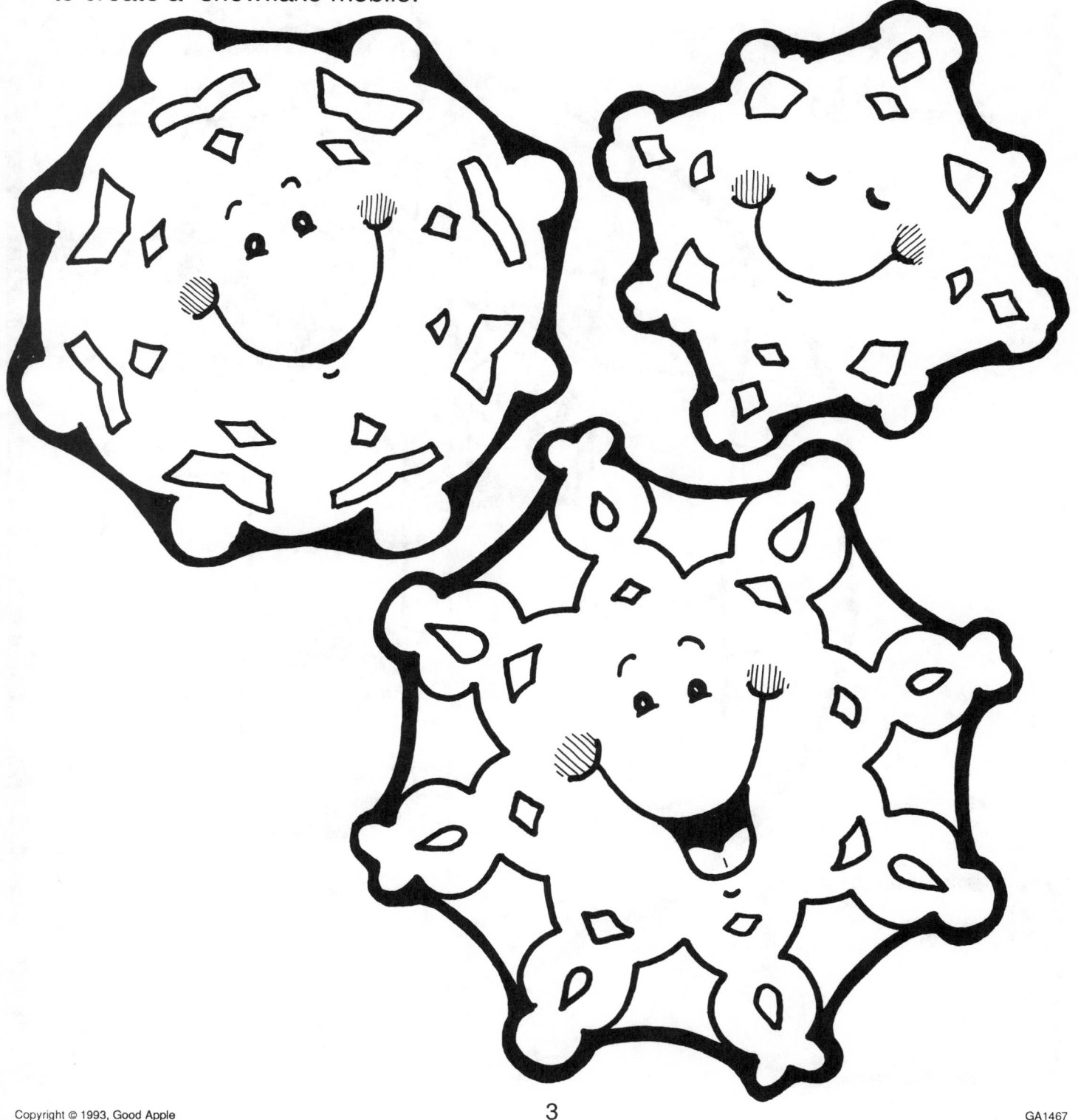

GA1467

Igloo

Reproduce igloo and ice block patterns on white paper. Cut out and mount igloo on light blue construction paper. Finish the igloo by pasting the ice blocks over the Eskimo and polar bear.

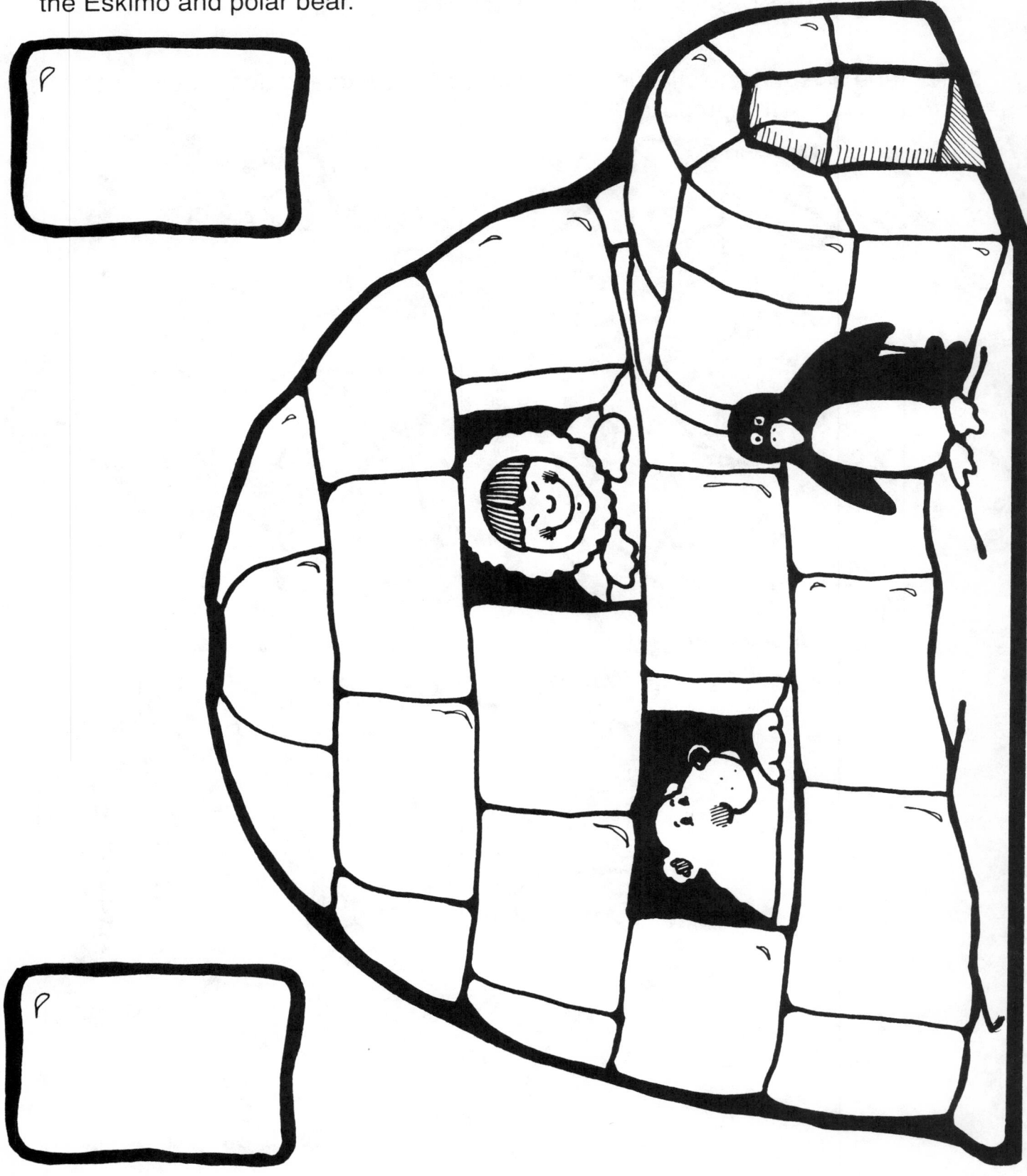

GA1467

Penguin

Reproduce the penguin and wing patterns on page 6. Color and cut out on the heavy outlines. Attach the wing to the penguin with a metal paper fastener, matching the circles. Reproduce the ice pattern on this page on light blue paper; cut out on the heavy outline. Glue to the penguin's feet, as illustrated. The penguin may also be mounted on a 9" x 12" (22.86 x 30.48 cm) sheet of blue construction paper.

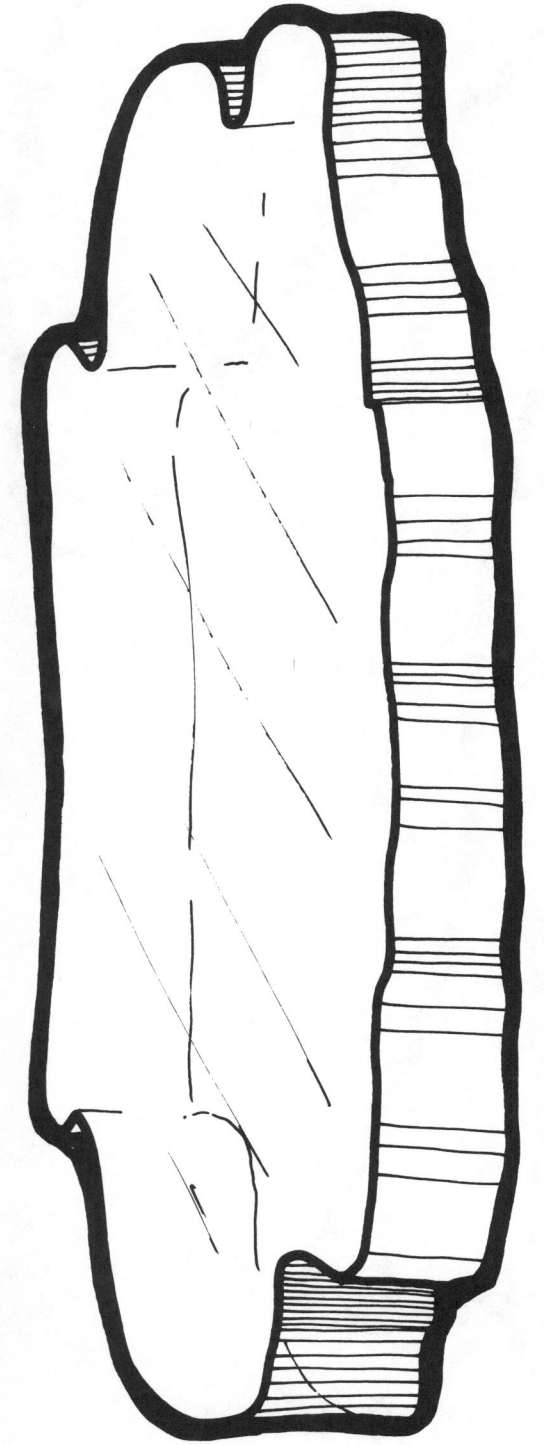

Penguin

GA1467

My Mittens

Reproduce the patterns on this page and page 8 on plain or colored paper. Color and decorate with stickers or drawings. Cut out on the heavy outlines. Tape a small length of colorful yarn to the back of each mitten to join.

7

My Mittens

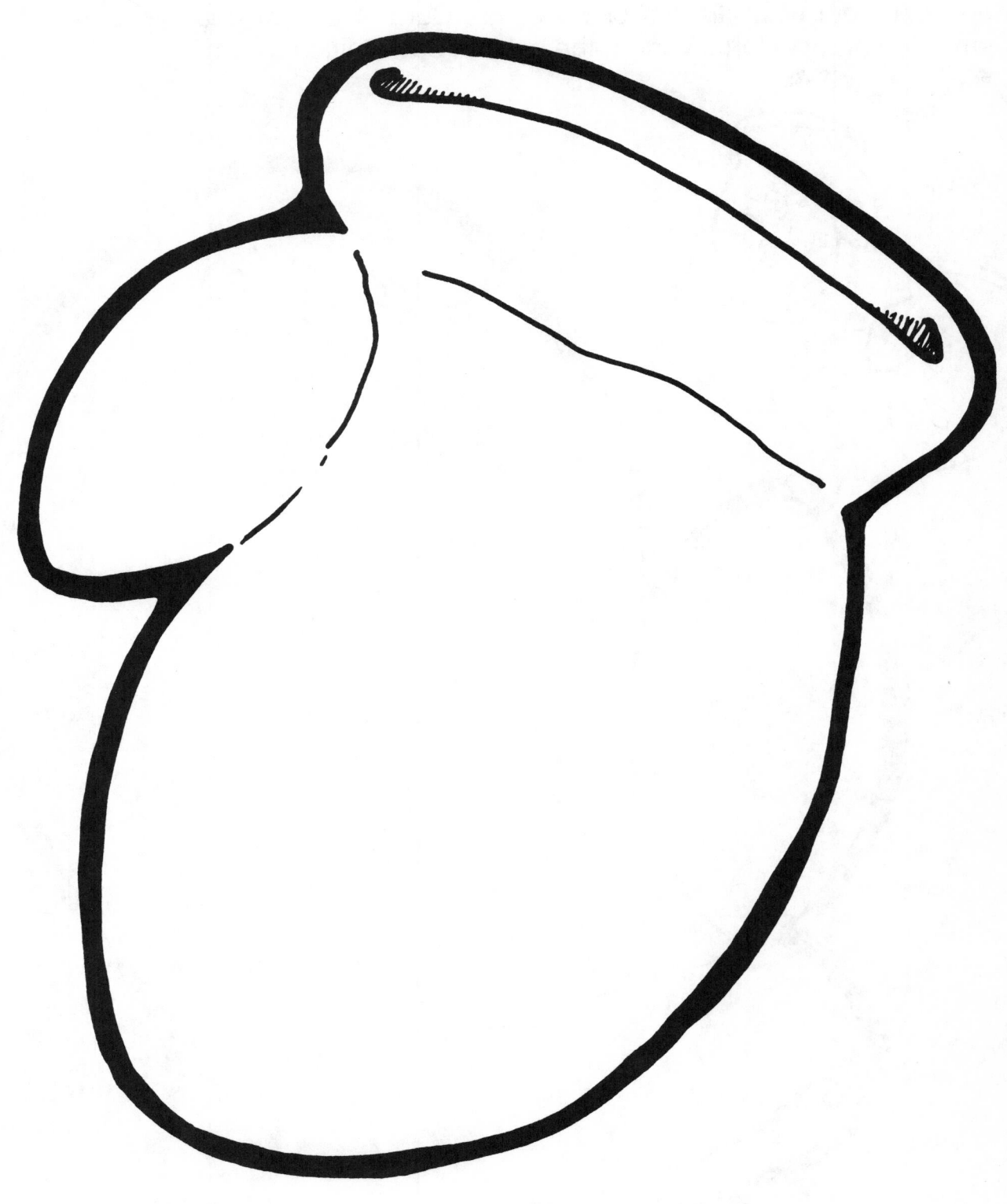

8

GA1467

Thermometer

Reproduce the pattern below. Cut out on the heavy outline. Locate the temperature on the thermometer and color the graph area red from the bottom oval until you reach that figure.

GA1467

Gingerbread Boy

Reproduce the pattern below on heavy dark brown paper. Cut out on the heavy outline. Decorate as desired with glue and glitter, wrapping paper, yarn, markers, etc.

GA1467

Gingerbread Girl

Reproduce the pattern below on heavy dark brown paper. Cut out on the heavy outline. Decorate as desired with glue and glitter, wrapping paper, yarn, markers, etc.

GA1467

Gingerbread House

Reproduce the pattern below on heavy tan paper. Color and cut out on the heavy outline. Run a thin line of white glue along the areas you want frosted. Sprinkle with white or crystal glitter. Punch out the hole with a paper punch and tie with a colorful piece of string to make a hanger.

GA1467

Candy Cane

Reproduce the pattern below on heavy paper. Have the children color each area with a heart red, and trace each dotted line with red. Cut out on the heavy outline.

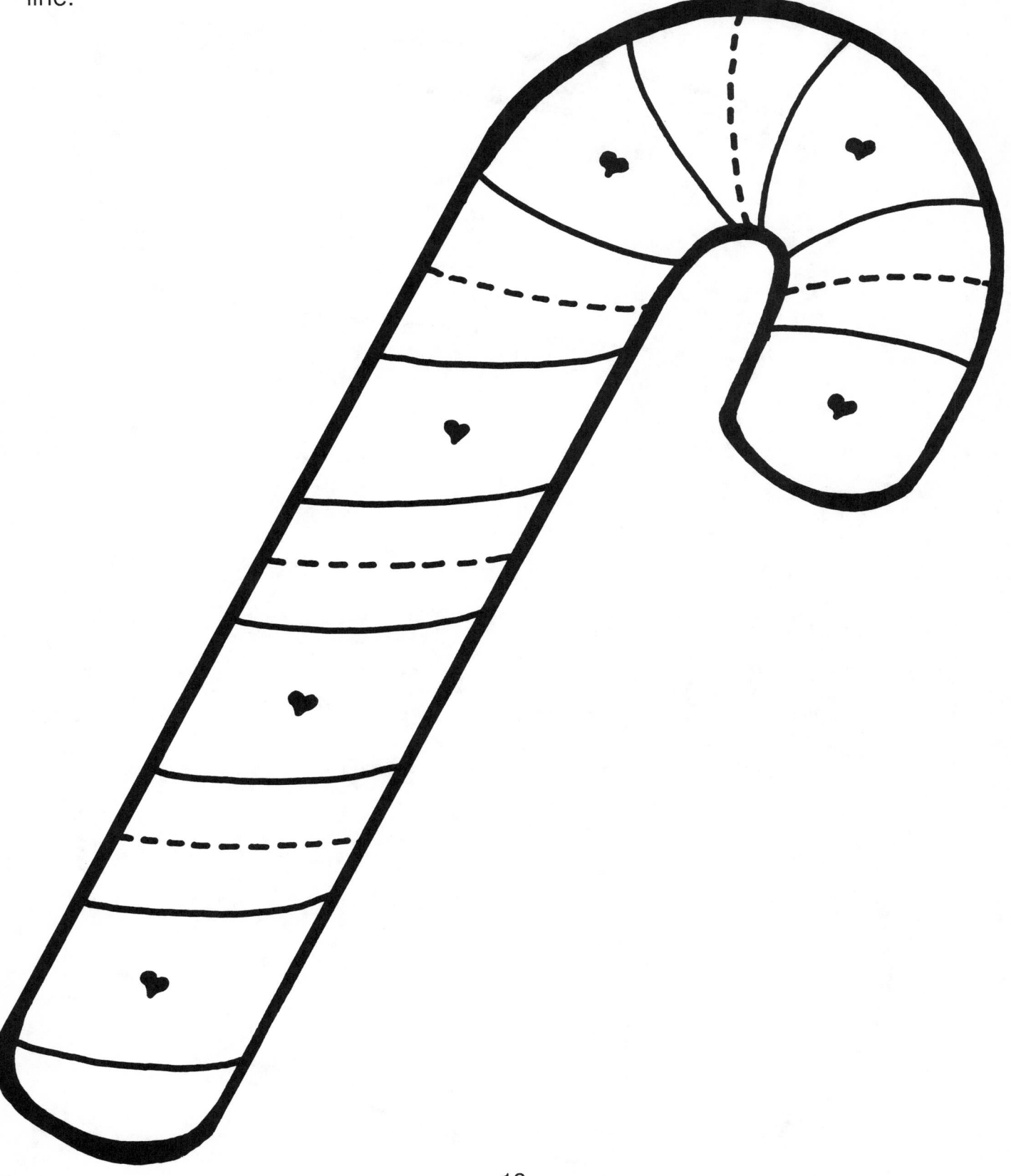

Stocking

Reproduce the pattern below. Cut out the stocking on the heavy outline. Personalize the cuff with the child's name. Decorate with crayons, markers and glitter as desired.

14

GA1467

Christmas Tree

Reproduce the pattern below on white or light green paper. Color and cut out on the heavy outline. Decorate the tree with stick-on stars, glitter, sequins, cereal or other decorations such as stickers.

GA1467

Wreath

Reproduce the pattern below on heavy paper. Color and cut out on the heavy outline. Decorate the wreath by pasting on sequins, cereal, buttons, shapes cut from wrapping paper, etc. Mount on an 8½" x 8½" (21.6 x 21.6 cm) sheet of red paper, if desired.

Toy Bag

Reproduce the pattern on page 18 on tan paper. Color the rope and cut out on the heavy outline. Reproduce the toys pattern below, color and cut out. Paste inside the toy bag. You may also reproduce the toy bag only (on white paper) and have children draw their own toys "inside" the bag. Color and cut out. Mount on 9" x 12" (22.86 x 30.48 cm) construction paper, if desired.

17

GA1467

Toy Bag

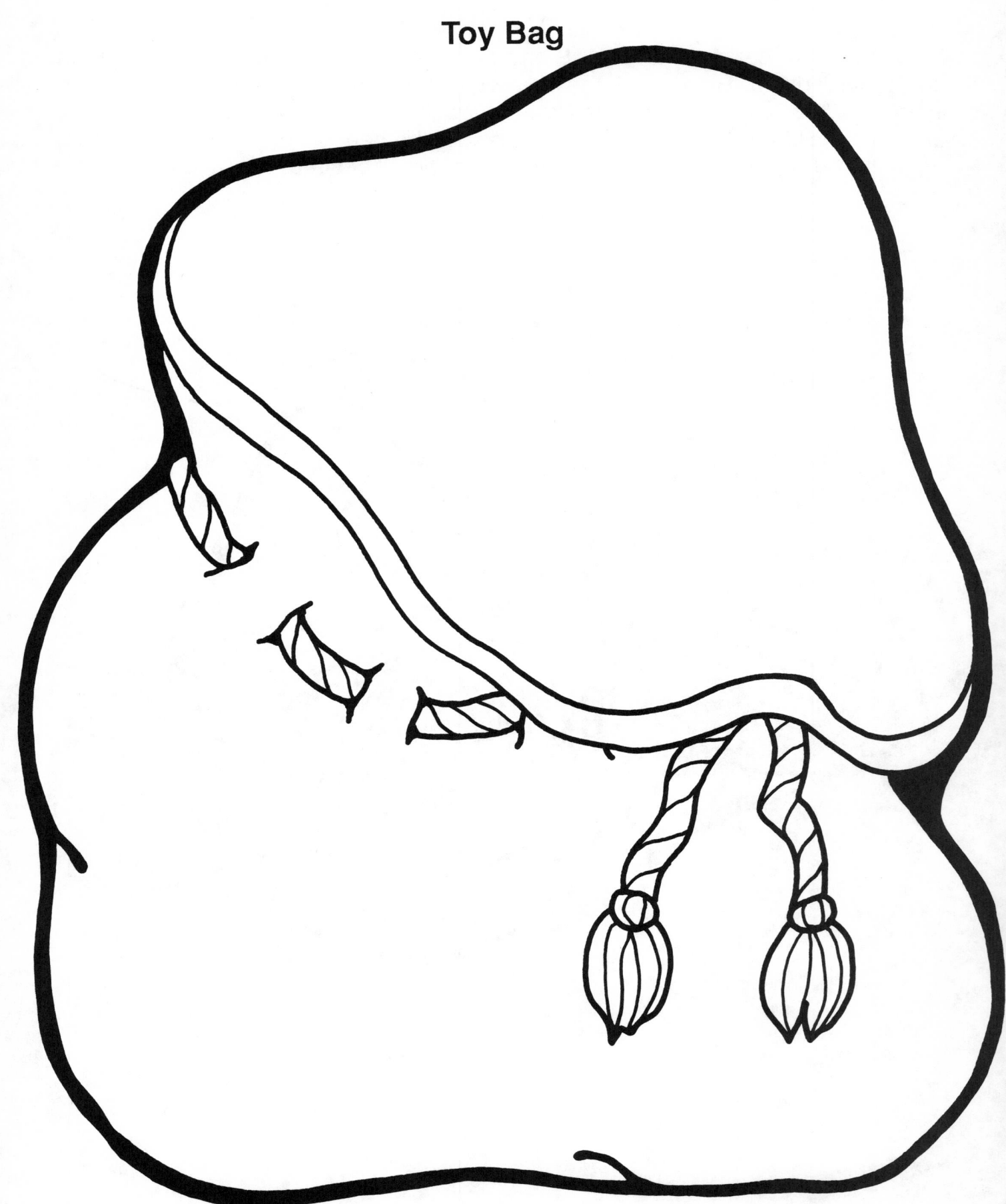

18

Reindeer

Reproduce the patterns on this page and page 20. Color and cut out on the heavy outlines. Glue the pattern pieces together, as illustrated.

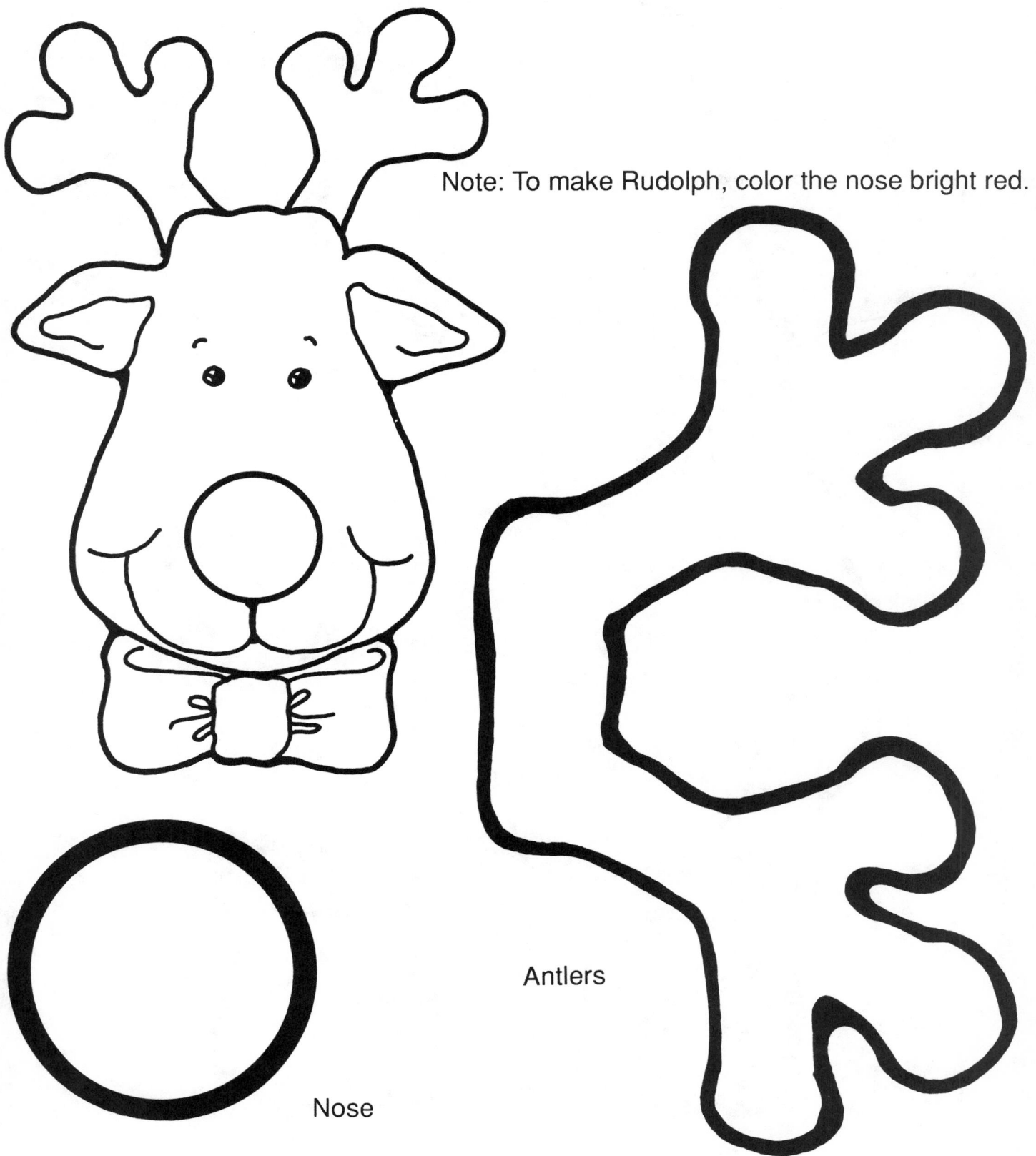

Note: To make Rudolph, color the nose bright red.

Antlers

Nose

19

GA1467

Reindeer

GA1467

Santa Stand-up

Reproduce the pattern below on heavy paper. Color and cut out on the heavy outline. Glue a cardboard tube (that has been colored or covered with paper) to the back of the Santa, as illustrated. You may also glue a small wrapped candy cane to the stick Santa is carrying.

"Welcome Santa" Door Hanger

Reproduce this pattern on heavy paper. Color and cut out on the heavy outline. Add the child's name in the banner. Decorate with dots of glitter if desired.

Cookies for Santa

Reproduce the cookies below. Color* and cut out on the heavy outlines. Paste cookies to a paper plate as illustrated.

*You may also "decorate" the cookies with glue and glitter.

GA1467

Santa Letter

Reproduce the letter below on plain or cream-colored paper. Color and decorate with bits of glitter, if desired. Cut out on the heavy outline and fill in or send home with children to share with family.

Note: Dab edges of letter with strong tea to create an antique look.

Mini Holiday Cards

Reproduce the cards below and on page 26. Color, cut out and fold on the solid line. Write a holiday message inside each card. You may also punch a hole in the upper left corner of the folded card and tie a string through the hole to make a gift tag.

GA1467

Mini Holiday Cards

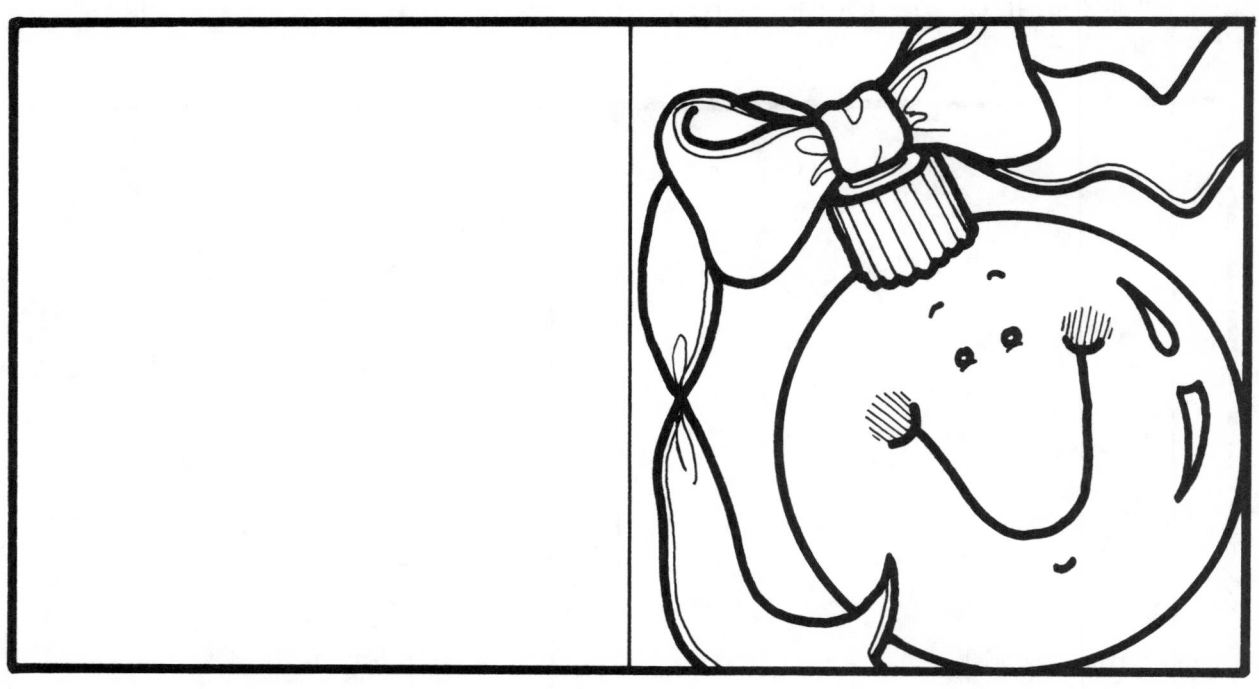

GA1467

Hanukkah Poster and Dreidel Chain

For Poster: Reproduce the pattern on page 28. Using the triangle pattern below, cut two triangles out of blue construction paper. Glue the first triangle to the solid-lined area on the poster. Glue the second triangle to the dotted-line area.

For Dreidel Chain: Reproduce the patterns below on heavy paper. Color and cut out on the heavy outlines. Punch out the holes with a paper punch and attach the dreidels together with paper clips to form a chain.

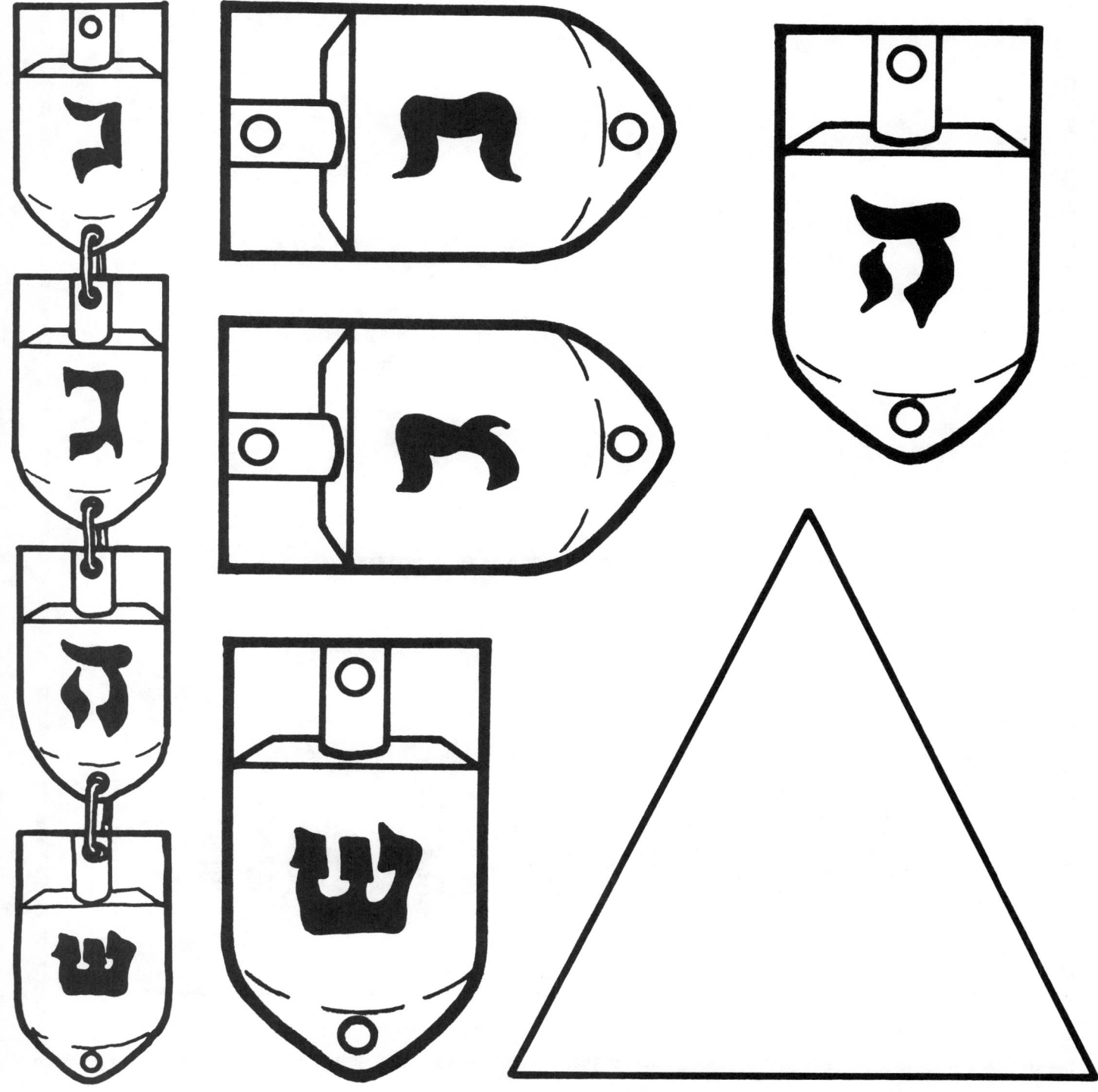

GA1467

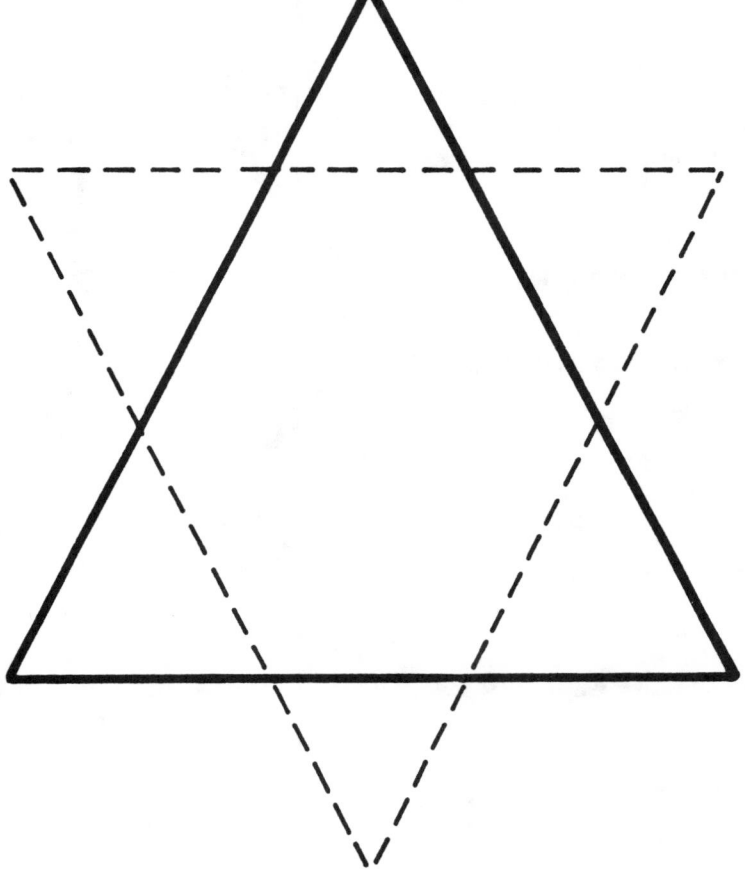

Happy

Hanukkah

GA1467

Kwanzaa

Reproduce the pattern below. Cut out on the heavy outline. Have the children color the center candle on the Kinara black. Color the three left candles red, the three right green. Color the rest of the picture.

GA1467

New Year's Party

Reproduce and enlarge the pattern on this page. Color and cut out on the heavy outline. Cut a strip of paper 8$\frac{1}{2}$" x 1$\frac{1}{4}$" (21.6 x 2.6 cm). On one side decorate with colorful crayons, pencils or markers. Wrap the strip tightly around a pencil with the decorated side out, and hold for a few seconds to create a paper curl, illustrated below. Spread glue or paste over the square as indicated on the pattern and attach the end of the paper curl to it to create a 3-D "noisemaker."

Note: You may also reproduce this on heavier weight paper and glue a real 1$\frac{1}{2}$" (3.8 cm) yarn pom-pom to the top of the party hat, or glue bits of real confetti or streamers to the picture.

HAPPY
NEW
YEAR!

Paste
Paper
Here

Attach this end to pattern

Curl around pencil

Chinese New Year Dragon Mask

Place the pattern below on a folded sheet of colorful construction paper. Cut out, following the pattern. Punch out the holes with a paper punch and reinforce the backs of the holes, if desired. Tie with colorful yarn and decorate with markers, feathers, glitter, etc.

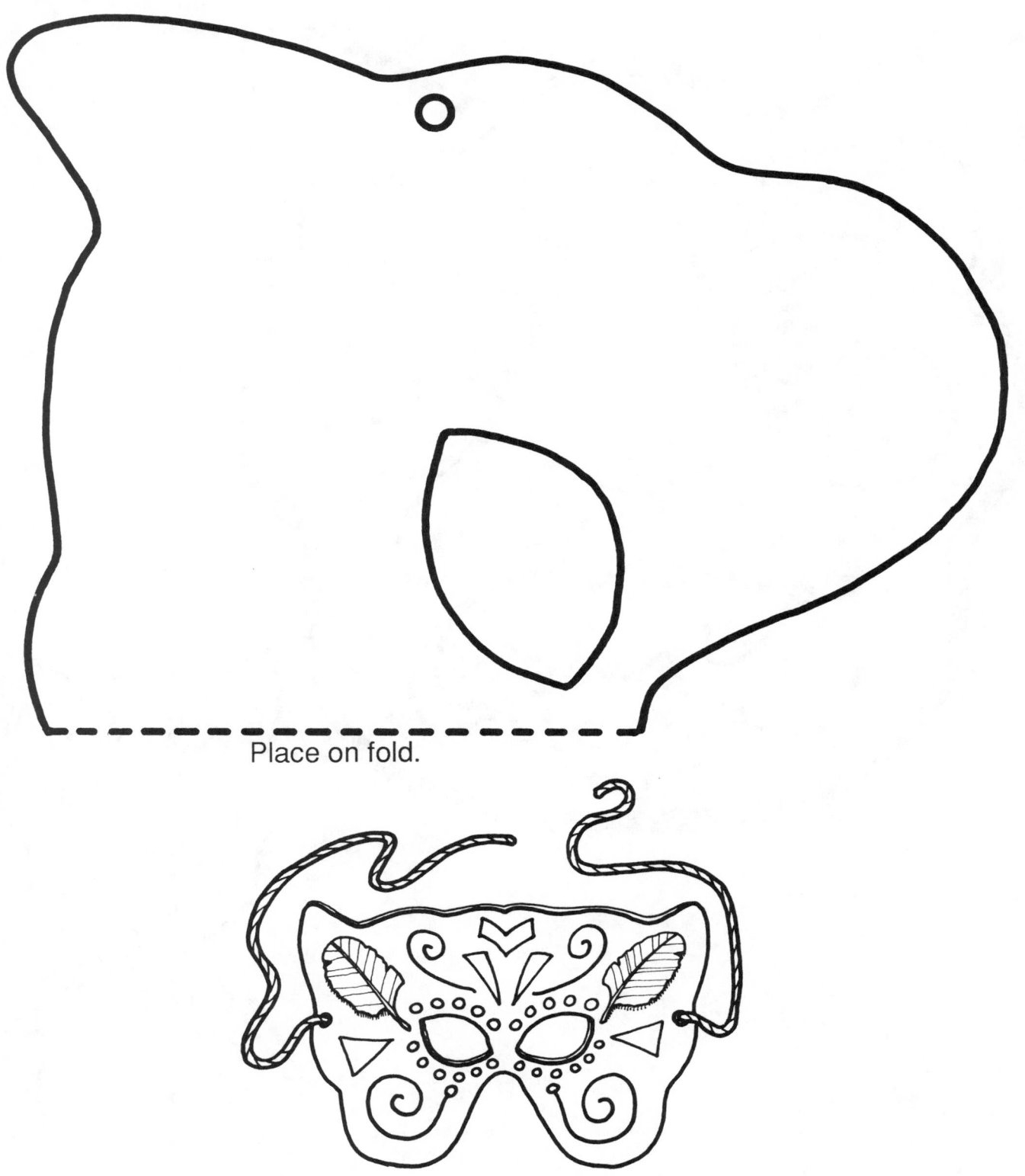

Place on fold.

31

Chinese New Year Puppet

Reproduce the pattern below on heavy paper. Color and cut out on the heavy outline. Decorate with glitter and ribbons if desired and glue a wide craft stick to the back of the puppet, as illustrated.

32

GA1467

Martin Luther King, Jr.

Reproduce the pattern below on heavy paper. Cut out on the heavy outline and

1. Glue a wide craft stick to the back, or
2. Glue a 1" (2.54 cm) piece of straw to the back and thread a piece of yarn or string through it to make a necklace, as illustrated.

GA1467

Lincoln and Washington Stick Puppets

Reproduce the patterns below on heavy paper. Color and cut out on the heavy outlines. Glue or tape a craft stick to the back of the figures, as illustrated.

Abraham Lincoln

George Washington

GA1467

Washington and Lincoln Mini Books

Reproduce the mini booklets on plain or colored paper. Cut out and color, if desired. Fold back on the dotted lines and forward on the solid lines as illustrated. Staple the left edge as shown.

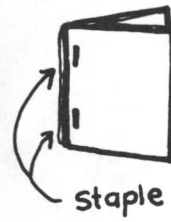

staple

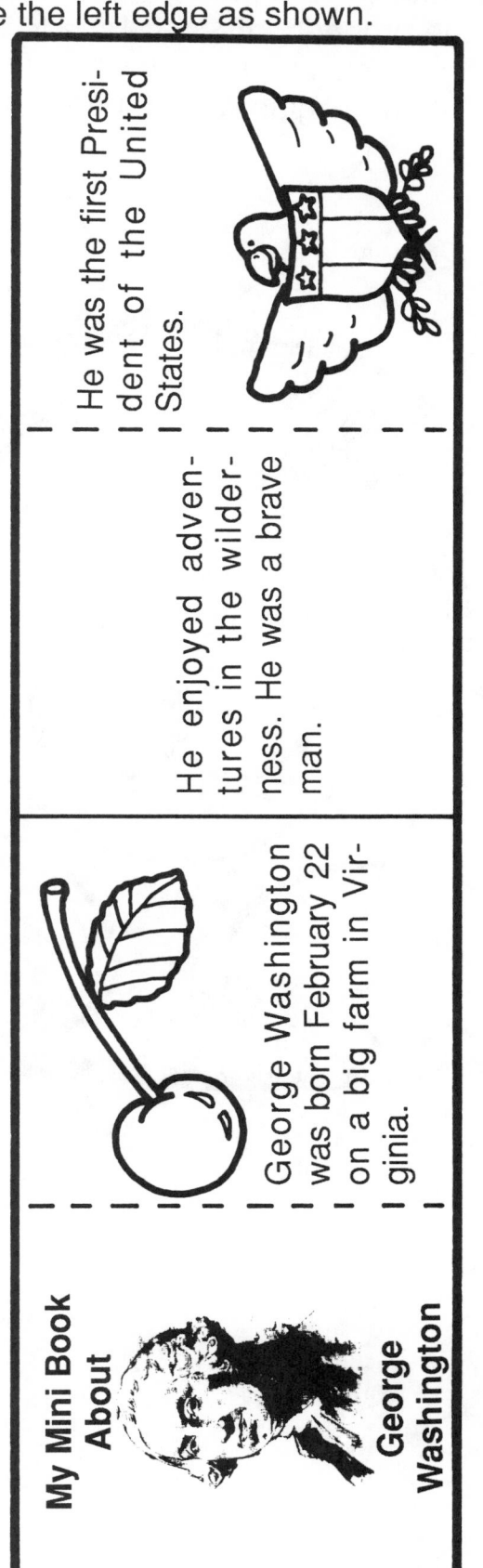

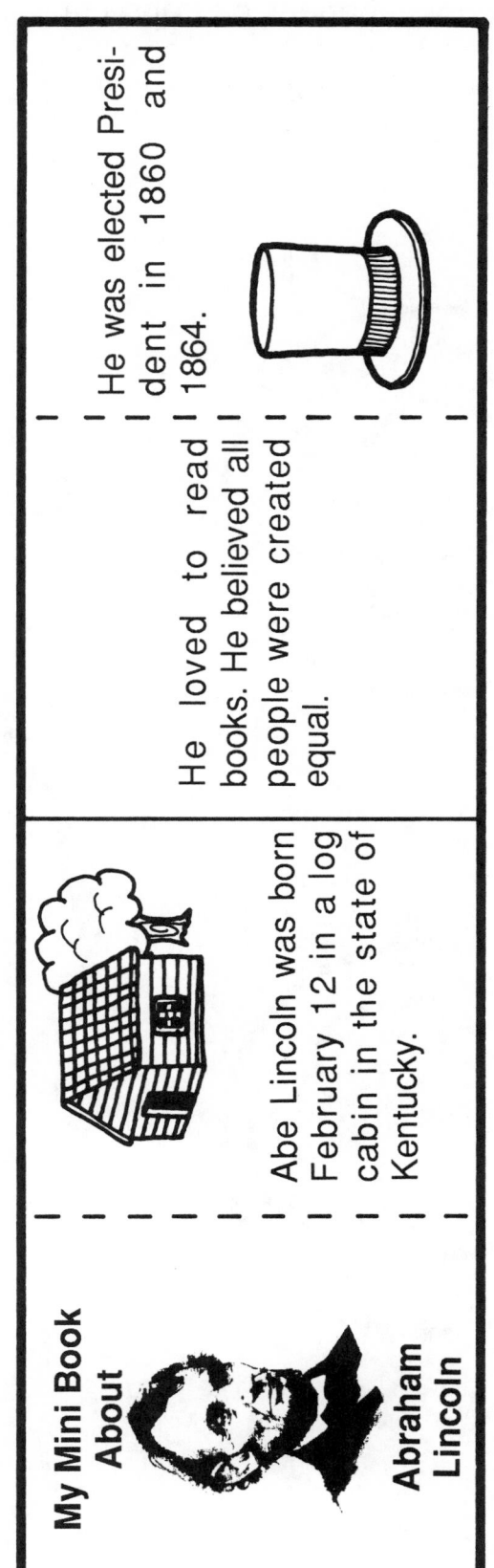

GA1467

Groundhog Day

Reproduce the pattern on page 37. Reproduce the weather and groundhog patterns on this page. Color and cut out. If the groundhog saw its shadow, glue the groundhog above its den and the sun in the circle above. Color the shadow grey or black. If the groundhog didn't see its shadow, glue the groundhog above its den, but glue the cloud in the circle and don't color the shadow. Mark an *X* in the correct box.

The groundhog ☐ did ☐ did not see its shadow.

Happy Valentine

Reproduce the patterns below on white, red or pink heavy paper. Cut out on the heavy outline, and punch out the holes with a paper punch. Insert a 6" (15.24 cm) piece of pipe cleaner in each of the holes and tape on the back. Tape a hand to the other end of the pipe cleaners as illustrated. Attach a Valentine or notice to the hands, if desired.

38

GA1467

Pocketful of Love

Reproduce the patterns on this page and page 40. You may wish to use pink paper. Color, if desired, and cut out the heart on the heavy outline. Cut the cards apart. Attach the pocket to the heart back with staples or a small edge of glue. Punch out the holes and tie with ribbon or yarn to form a hanger. Place the cards in the pocket.

 **This coupon is good for 1 (one) HUG!**

 **This coupon is good for 1 (one) COMPLIMENT.**

 **This coupon is good for 1 (one) BIG SMILE!**

 **This coupon is good for**

_____

Fill in.

A Pocketful of Love for You!

GA1467

Valentine Holder

Reproduce the pattern below on white or pink paper. Color, decorate with glitter if desired and cut out on the heavy outline. Add name and glue to the front of a white, lunch-sized paper bag. Add a bow above the sign.

valentines

TO
TEDDY

FOR MY
FRIEN

HAP
VALEN
DAY!

I
LIK
YOU!

Be
MY
Valentine

BE
FRIENDS

Chelsea's
valentines

This Award Is Presented to

_____
name

For "Beary" Good Work!
Congratulations!

Signed

Date

42

Winter

Newsletter/Parent Letter Border

GA1467

Patterns for Winter

Big Activities for Little Hands

Contents:

File Folder Cover